BROKEN HOME

ISBN# 978-1-998532-19-3

1. Christianity 2. Devotions 3. Holy Bible 4. Meditation

Printed in the United States of America
Published in the United States of America

www.aheliapublishing.org
support@aheliapublishing.org

Ahelia Publishing

BROKEN HOME

AUSTIN FRENCH

And let us not grow weary of doing good, for in due season we will reap, if we do not give up.

Galatians 6:9

Index

1. A Moment in time
2. Healing from the Inside Out
3. Forgiven and Free
4. Growing in Brokenness
5. Sweet Grace
6. Hope in Heartache
7. Up From the Ashes
8. Strength of Vulnerability
9. God's Love in Unlovely Places
10. Building Bridges, Not Walls
11. The Gift of the Struggle
12. Forgiveness: A Path to Healing
13. Embracing Imperfection
14. Grace for Every Scar
15. Creating a New Legacy
16. Faithful in the Fractures
17. The God of Second Chances
18. Becoming Who You Were Meant to Be
19. When Home Hurts
20. The Beauty of a Scar
21. Embracing Change
22. No Longer Weary
23. The Promise of Restoration
24. Faith in the Storm
25. The Goodness of God in Every Season
26. Hope Amidst the Trials
27. The Depths of His Affection
28. Rooted in His Love
29. Everlasting Embrace
30. Growth from Grief
31. Abiding in the Vine
32. This is Not the End
33. He is Faithful
34. The Goodness of God
35. An Anchor in the Storm
36. God Sees
37. Trusting God With Your Story
38. God in the Broken
39. Choosing Thoughts
40. God Says

A Moment in Time

For I know the plans I have for you, declares the LORD, plans for welfare and not for evil, to give you a future and a hope.

Jeremiah 29:11

Life can sometimes seem as though you have no control over your own destiny. Others can make choices that affect you, and you watch as your hopes vanish like a vapor. You can cry that life is unfair, and absolutely, it often is! God never promised fairness in this world.

Life was unfair for Jesus, Paul, Joseph, Esther, and Moses, just to name a few. However, God wrote their stories just as He has written yours. He knows you as He knows them.

It is easy to forget that your life's story is just that: an entire lifetime of days, hours, minutes, joys and sorrows, events and experiences. But in each of those, God is leading you toward hope and a future with Him— an eternity with Him. There is no greater hope than that realization that even though your days on this earth may be rippled with moments—some amazing and others terrible—each one is leading you toward Him.

He knows the plans for your life because He is already there. He is in your past, present, and future. In His incredible wisdom, God sometimes allows you to face difficult days and teaches you to come to Him. Hard days beckon you to seek Him, rest in Him, cry out to Him, trust His ways, and seek His Word.

Better days allow time and space to catch your breath, enjoy His goodness, count your blessings, and look back to see exactly how He led, taught, and grew you. He is in all your moments and promises you a future and hope. You can count on that every day.

PRAY & BELIEVE

FFather, You are God; I am not. When I am undone by the unfairness of this life, remind me that in pain, there is purpose. Seal on my mind that life is a compilation of moments, and they each lead me closer to You. Strengthen my heart to take another step, even when my flesh screams to give up. You have not forgotten my moments in time. You are in each of them. Remind me daily that in the hard moments, You are as near as in the easy ones. Thank you for giving me moments with You. Let me hear Your voice calling me into each one. Amen.

PAUSE TO CONSIDER HIM

Think back to a moment in life when you didn't see how you'd make it through, but now you can see that God was writing your story and did it better than you could have. Pause and consider how He not only rescued you, but you grew because of it:

_____
_____
_____
_____
_____
_____
_____
_____

How are you a better person today because of what you learned in that experience?

_____
_____
_____
_____
_____
_____
_____

What is your take-away from this lesson?

_____
_____
_____
_____
_____
_____

I Praise You For

-
-
-

Healing from the Inside Out

He heals the brokenhearted and binds up their wounds.

Psalm 147:3

God sees our pain. Many days, it feels as though He is far away and doesn't notice our suffering. However, feelings can be misleading. It is a wise person who knows how to separate feelings from truth. Yet, when confronted with the agony this world can inflict, our emotions are loud and demand attention. We feel them profoundly and, left on our own, are unable to take control or even think with a clear head.

The Bible does not suggest that we will never face pain or that our hearts will never break. Jesus' heart often broke as He witnessed the suffering of others. Yet, we somehow believe we should be spared from the deep pain that can afflict the heart.

While God never promised we would avoid all pain, He did promise to bind up our wounds. He is faithful to keep that promise, no matter how deep the wound. God is wise; He never leaves us in our brokenness. Even if we find ourselves slumped on the floor, questioning why things happen as they do, that does not keep Him from coming close, pulling us into His heart, and healing our pain.

Strangely enough, it is during these broken moments—whether they last days or years—that we often feel God's presence most tangibly. He is near to the brokenhearted. In the midst of our heartache, God gets down on the floor where we cry and sits with us. He cries with us, understands us, and then reaches out to touch the parts of us that are shattered, gently repairing them.

The scars may remain for a lifetime, but as the Lord binds the brokenness, the healing will come.

PRAY & BELIEVE

Some days, I feel so shattered inside, especially as I remember things from my past when I was hurt. Lord, I wonder if You were broken as You saw me be broken? I think You cried when I cried. But those days are so far gone now; I want to be healed from them. Father, even though the scars remain, I know the pain doesn't have to. Will You remove it from me? When I want to grab it back, please remind me that I don't want it back. It's not good for me to keep picking it up, so even if it takes a thousand times, Lord, remind me to leave it with You and trust that You are capable of healing my heart. Amen.

PAUSE TO CONSIDER HIM

Think back to a moment in life when you didn't see how you'd make it through, but now you can see that God was writing your story and did it better than you could have. Pause and consider how He not only rescued you, but you grew because of it:

_____
_____
_____
_____
_____
_____
_____
_____

How are you a better person today because of what you learned in that experience?

_____
_____
_____
_____
_____
_____
_____

What is your take-away from this lesson?

_____
_____
_____
_____
_____
_____

I Praise You For

-
-
-

Forgiven and Free

So if the Son sets you free, you will be free indeed.

John 8:36

Sometimes, the fewest words carry the most power; that is what we find in this scripture of only a dozen words. The message? Freedom!

In our world, freedom is not only challenging to find; it's hard to even describe, yet it is something we all desire and fight for. What is freedom really? Does it give us the license to do whatever we please? It cannot mean such a thing because, by common sense, that would infer my freedom would, at some point, impede your freedom. We cannot both do whatever we want at any given time and still both remain free. It must mean something else.

Upon thinking deeper on these dozen words, this scripture indicates that to be free indeed, we must first be set free by the One who holds the keys to such. And if, as indicated, we are set free, then we can no longer be burdened by whatever the opposite of freedom is. One cannot be free and bound at the same time.

This freedom is life-changing. Paul and Silas were free while in prison, indicating that this freedom comes from within, not without. We are free to forgive, show grace, love mercy, offer kindness, sacrifice, and bless those who are undeserving of such. This freedom is to be unrestricted—to be Christ-like. This freedom is a soul freedom against which there are no restraints.

There is only one way to achieve this freedom, and that is to be set free from the chains of the old nature: the flesh. When we walk in the Spirit, we are free. When we live in the flesh, no freedom can be found. Has the Son of God set you free? Then you are free indeed!

PRAY & BELIEVE

Father, I don't feel free consistently. Too often, my soul feels tired and burdened by memories, feelings, and fears rearing their ugly head. I desire to live in this freedom where no person can take it. Lord, give me wisdom to know how to walk in this freedom. The scripture says if You set me free, then I am free. I want to be free from my past, and all that comes with it. I choose it, Lord. I hold it tightly and fight the desire to return to its chains. Give me the courage to do so. Amen.

PAUSE TO CONSIDER HIM

Where in your life do you feel the most free? Where do you feel the most bound? How can you begin to take the bound areas and move them to the areas of freedom? Are you ready and willing to let go of those ones that are holding you?

_____
_____
_____
_____
_____
_____
_____

How does letting go of the areas where you are bound bring freedom?

_____
_____
_____
_____
_____
_____

What is your take-away from this lesson?

_____
_____
_____
_____
_____
_____

I Praise You For

-
-
-

Growing in Brokenness

But he said to me, "My grace is sufficient for you, for my power is made perfect in weakness." Therefore I will boast all the more gladly of my weaknesses, so that the power of Christ may rest upon me.

2 Corinthians 12:9

Weakness is underrated. As humans, we work hard to ensure we are strong. Physically, we go to the gym; mentally, we read self-help books; and spiritually, we listen to podcasts and attend church. But then, something happens in life for which we were unprepared, and our strength vanishes. What now?

Family breakups are one of those that, as children, we have no control over. We get no say. Nobody asks our opinion. We are lost and broken, and often, adults are distracted by their own brokenness, limiting their capacity to know how to deal with their children's pain.

But God sees the littlest ones, the ones without a voice, and He scoops us up and holds us tight. He is our protector, our victor, our champion. God is our strength when ours is long gone. He shows up when others are MIA. He never breaks a promise.

We might think we must be strong for everyone else, and perhaps that's true, but our strength is a vapor—here one minute and gone the next. God's strength remains steadfast; His strength becomes ours.

Weakness is the breeding ground for growth. In pain, we cry to the Lord and find His grace is all-sufficient. He gets us through. Christ is close to the broken, so let's stop pretending to be strong and start believing that our weakness opens the door for Christ's strength to step in and change us from the inside out. Our situation may not change, but we will be changed, causing the situation to pale in the light of God's grace.

PRAY & BELIEVE

God, I do not want to be weak or broken. I don't want to have the memories that haunt me. I don't want to come from a broken home. But none of that was my choice, so I am coming to You with all the broken pieces. I know You will take all that has broken me down and use it to make me strong for the right reasons. Lord, take what was meant for evil and turn it to good so that I can help others who maybe don't know of Your strength, in so doing, become whole and unburdened. Let me be satisfied in my weakness, knowing it will produce your strength. Amen.

PAUSE TO CONSIDER HIM

Where in your life do you feel weak and vulnerable? Can you invite the Lord into that place and trust Him to be your strength? Can you let go of the lie that you need to be strong for everyone else and allow them find their strength in the Lord?

_____
_____
_____
_____
_____
_____
_____

How might your life be better if you embrace weakness and let Christ be your strength?

_____
_____
_____
_____
_____
_____

What is your take-away from this lesson?

_____
_____
_____
_____
_____
_____

I Praise You For

-
-
-

Sweet Grace

The LORD is gracious and merciful, slow to anger
and abounding in steadfast love. The LORD is good to
all, and his mercy is over all that he has made.

Psalm 145:8-9

Not everyone knows this kind of grace. Many of us grew up in homes where one or both of our parents were easily angered, and their love was conditional. Certainly, grace was not often offered.

I knew of a young man who was a world champion in his sport, but after an injury ended his career, he was suddenly faced with an identity crisis. I recall him telling me that for most of his life, his dad referred to him by his sport rather than his name. His father treated him differently when he won than when he lost. But now that he no longer played, his Olympic hopes gone; this young man had no idea who he was.

We often see God as we see our own fathers. If we happened to have an excellent dad who protected us, loved us without condition, and quickly forgave us for our mistakes, that is how we see God. But, if, on the other hand, our father was gruff, rough, or absent, or if we had to perform to gain his attention and excel to keep it, that is how we tend to see God.

But we must put on different glasses to clearly see our Heavenly Father. This scripture gives us a glimpse into His kindness toward us. He is slow to anger and quick to forgive. Our Heavenly Father abounds in steadfast love—unconditional love. His love toward us does not depend one iota on us. We cannot earn it, nor do we deserve it. He is gracious and merciful, slow to anger, and good to us because of Him, not because of us. If we cannot earn it, then we cannot lose it. It's all because of Him. Believe it, receive it, and trust Him.

PRAY & BELIEVE

Oh God, I want to reach out and take hold of this kind of love. This has not been my experience, but I want it to be. Even though my earthly parents were flawed, and my childhood was less than perfect, You are not flawed. You are the perfect Father. Open my heart to receive this kind of grace, and let how You see me become my identity. You are good; of this, I am sure. Thank you that Your love depends on You, the Perfect One, not me. Remind me in times of trouble that I cannot lose Your love, and You will never fail me. Amen.

PAUSE TO CONSIDER HIM

Where did your own parents let you down? Can you forgive them, realizing they are human and imperfect? How can you let go of their failings and replace them with the perfect love of the Heavenly Father? What does your identity in Christ look like?

_____
_____
_____
_____
_____
_____
_____
_____

Where can you make changes to be a better parent, friend, sibling, child, or spouse?

_____
_____
_____
_____
_____
_____
_____

What is your take-away from this lesson?

_____
_____
_____
_____
_____
_____
_____

I Praise You For

-
-
-

Hope in Heartache

May the God of hope fill you with all joy and peace in believing,
so that by the power of the Holy Spirit you may abound in hope.

Romans 15:13

To understand this scripture, we must dissect and examine it carefully. When we understand the words individually, we can internalize the message of the whole and once again abound in hope—even in heartache.

Joy, peace, and hope are usually thought of as emotions. So many Believers struggle to *find joy*. However, this is because they don't understand that joy is not a feeling but a steadfastness of faith. One walking in joy does not waver; they are not up one day and down the next. That person is steady, unwavering, day to day. The excitement that comes once in a while is just that: excitement.

Peace is similar in nature. It is not a feeling of euphoria but rather a state of mind that comes from trusting God. We see that in this Scripture, the phrase is *all joy and peace in believing*. The last word here that requires deeper thought is hope. What is hope? Can we hope in the circumstances? Should we place our hope in others? Surely not! The only One in whom we should place our hope is God.

I know too many who have hoped their family would be unbroken, that the parents would reconcile, and that they would not be stuck in the middle. However, when this does not happen, those who hope become angry at God. Their hope was not in God; it was in people, and people sometimes fail us. What they had was not hope, but a desire.

But hope! Hope is found in God, which is why we can have great hope in the middle of heartache. We hope in God to keep us, shelter us, and heal our hearts, and know that regardless of our feelings or whether He delivers us from the circumstances, He will never let us down.

PRAY & BELIEVE

Father, thank you for Your truth. I praise You that it is You who fills, and I who gets full. If it were not for You, I'd have no way to walk in peace or joy! But You, Lord, are so good, and I thank You for it. Please increase the work of the Holy Spirit in my life so that my joy might be overflowing and my hope would be steadfast. Remind me that these are not feelings to rise and fall but steadfast truths in knowing and trusting You. Please fill my heart with hope and deliver me from my own thoughts that get in the way. Keep my mind on You, the author of my life. Amen.

PAUSE TO CONSIDER HIM

Where were you placing hope that ended up bringing pain? Can you look back and see your hope was misplaced? It was in humans, not in God. Today, can you place your hope in God, knowing He will work all things together for your good?

_____
_____
_____
_____
_____
_____
_____

How did you feel when your hope was shattered? Can you hope in God?

_____
_____
_____
_____
_____
_____

What is your take-away from this lesson?

_____
_____
_____
_____
_____
_____

I Praise You For

-
-
-

Up From The Ashes

to grant to those who mourn in Zion—to give them a beautiful
headdress instead of ashes, the oil of gladness instead of mourning, the
garment of praise instead of a faint spirit; that they may be called oaks
of righteousness, the planting of the LORD, that he may be glorified.

Isaiah 61:3

Mourning lasts for a night, but joy comes in the morning. We all want joy without experiencing mourning; we'd far prefer the garment of praise instead of a heavy spirit, but in order to be called the oaks of righteousness so that He may be glorified, we must first walk through sorrow. I have always thought that we cannot understand one side of the equation without first understanding the other. What does that mean?

Simply put, one cannot rise from the ashes unless they've been in the fire. It is the fire that creates one of whom God is glorified. The heat burns off the residue and the sandpaper that files all the sharp edges into a smooth finish. None of us want to go through hardships, but adjusting our understanding of the "why" of such situations makes them a bit more bearable.

It is difficult to wrap our human brains around, but the truth is that we can only experience one side of the equation to the extent we have experienced the other: our joy will be as rich as our sadness is deep. Our fullness will be more treasured if we've been truly hungry. Do you get what I'm saying here? If we never felt grief, how could we understand praise?

God knows. He created us for His good pleasure so that He may be glorified in us. The Master does not cause us mourning but knows it will come. When it does, He will exchange it for gladness, and we will become strong in Him, and He will be glorified.

PRAY & BELIEVE

Father God, I don't want to be in the fire, and I don't want to experience the mourning. Regardless, I trust You. Expand my understanding of this, so the next time I feel like the sandpaper is grinding on my life, I will remember that there is a reason, and You will not allow the hard times to beat me up but will raise me from them. Set my feet on a rock, Lord, and don't allow the hard times to be too hard or the mourning to be too deep. Fill me with courage to press on, even when I want to give up. Remind me You are with me in the fire, and I will see Your goodness as You exchange it for gladness. Amen.

PAUSE TO CONSIDER HIM

Think back to a moment in life when you didn't see how you'd make it through, but now you can see that God was with you in the fire. Pause and consider how He not only rescued you, but you grew because of it:

_____
_____
_____
_____
_____
_____
_____

How are you a better person today because of what you learned in that experience?

_____
_____
_____
_____
_____
_____

What is your take-away from this lesson?

_____
_____
_____
_____
_____
_____

I Praise You For

-
-
-

Strength of Vulnerability

For the sake of Christ, then, I am content with weaknesses, insults, hardships, persecutions, and calamities. For when I am weak, then I am strong.

2 Corinthians 12:10

We are never stronger than when our human weakness has utterly failed us. This makes no sense in the human mind, but it is true. To be content in weakness seems lazy or confusing, as though when we are weak, we should do something.

That is the thing with humankind; we struggle to just be and let God be what we need. Our whole lives, we are told to do, attain, work toward, and in many things, we should. But when it comes to the weakness of our soul, God says, "Stop striving, stop struggling. Lean into Me. I have the strength you require."

The strength we need in the midst of struggle is one we cannot attain on our own. They are opposites. So, if we cannot find strength within ourselves, it must be found only in Christ.

The letting go can bring much peace of mind if we choose to allow ourselves to be content in weakness. When we let go of our striving, lift our hands and say, "God, I can't do it. I am weak. I need Your strength, Father," He answers. When we say these words, He steps in. He lifts us from the ashes of despair and supernaturally fills our souls with a deep and abiding inner strength.

People will see you and say, "How are you doing it? You are so strong." But you know that it is not you, but Him. His strength can bloom in the garden of your weakness. Trust Him and see the truth in this Scripture, and when you see He is faithful, you can finally exhale, lift your eyes, and know that, truly, you are content in your weakness.

PRAY & BELIEVE

When I am weak, which is so often, remind me not to focus on my situation but to turn my focus to You. Teach me how to lean on Your strength, Lord, without feeling guilty, like I should be doing something! I need Your strength so often. I want to rest and exhale, not carry the weight of the world, and my family, on my shoulders. Lord, teach me how! I can't do this on my own; I am weak. Draw me to You, teach me to abide there, at Your feet, and find rest in You. You are good to me, and I know You see me and my struggles. Open my eyes to see You and hear Your still, small voice. Amen.

PAUSE TO CONSIDER HIM

Where in my life do I feel weak and incapable? Do others require me to be strong? How can I take that expectation of others and turn it into a desire for the Lord? How can I lean into His strength and let go of the idea that I should be "doing something?"

_____
_____
_____
_____
_____
_____
_____

How will accepting my weaknesses make me into a better person?

_____
_____
_____
_____
_____
_____
_____

What is your take-away from this lesson?

_____
_____
_____
_____
_____
_____
_____

I Praise You For

God's Love in Unlovely Places

but God shows his love for us in that while we
were still sinners, Christ died for us.

Romans 5:8

When we think of love, certain ideas stir in our minds. Most, if not all of them, conjure up the idea of butterflies and warm, fuzzy feelings. Society has led us to believe that love is an emotion that one can fall into and also fall out of. But that is incorrect. Love is *not* a feeling. It can *cause* feelings now and then, but love, at its core, is an action, undriven by warm fuzzies or butterflies fluttering.

This is demonstrated no more clearly than Jesus' death on the cross. He did not do so because He was overcome with *feelings* of love and just could not help Himself. He chose the *action* of love. The scripture indicates His feelings were of deep sorrow; His actions were of love.

Understanding this truth makes this scripture all the more powerful. God *showed* His love for us—He put forth an action—that even while we were deep in our own sin, He chose the action of love by dying for us. When He looked across humanity past, present, and future, at the actions and sins of the world, I am sure we did not look all that loveable. But He did not take the action of love because we were loveable, but because He is love in action.

And while this is overwhelming and difficult for humans to grasp, it demonstrates the power of actions. We, too, must demonstrate love toward those who have hurt us, rejected us, and abandoned us, with the *action* of love. This might mean forgiving and praying for those who hurt us. This could include not retaliating or holding bitterness. Whatever the action might be, choose it. Choose to walk in love, whether you feel it or not. It will empower you and set you free.

PRAY & BELIEVE

Father, I am so thankful You chose the action of love. Thank you for looking at me and deciding that even in my filthy state, I was worth loving. You have rescued me from destruction, not because I earned it, but because You are good. Lord, I have held bitterness and unforgiveness toward those who have wounded me. I didn't deserve to be treated the way I was, but neither did You. Help me to let go of the emotions of the hurt and instead bless me with the courage to choose an action of love toward those. Help me to become more like You every day. Teach me to love based on choice, not on feelings. Amen.

PAUSE TO CONSIDER HIM

Who in my life do I hesitate to demonstrate love to? Why? Can I choose to take an action to show love? What might that action be? If I cannot do it on my own, can I trust the Lord to give me the strength to carry out that action? Why or why not?

_____
_____
_____
_____
_____
_____
_____

How are you a better person today because of God's demonstration of love?

_____
_____
_____
_____
_____
_____

What is your take-away from this lesson?

_____
_____
_____
_____
_____
_____

I Praise You For

-
-
-

Building Bridges, Not Walls

with all humility and gentleness, with patience, bearing with one another in love, eager to maintain the unity of the Spirit in the bond of peace.

Ephesians 4:2-3

Bearing with one another. What a phrase. Do we understand such an idea or what implementing this instruction requires? As a society, we don't bear with one another well. It's not something we hear sermons on, generally, and certainly, the age of social media is not a good breeding ground for it. Yet, we must build bridges and walk in unity.

Our first response to someone's poor decisions is judgment. But look at the power words used here. *Humility* and *gentleness*: these words leave no room for judgment or "I told you so." These words build bridges. With *patience and in love*: more words that build bridges to those we may rather want to erect a very thick, tall wall.

When we are hurt, we want to put our hands out and keep the ones who cause us pain far away. Our flesh screams and we naturally want to maintain distance from that one. We vow never to allow that person to hurt us again, and take steps to keep them out of our lives. But this Scripture suggests otherwise.

God wants His children to live in this manner, in the grace of this verse. He knows it is for our best that He suggests we bear with one another in love and gentleness, not throwing mud because we could each have mud thrown right back at us. We are all guilty of causing someone else pain to one degree or another. What a peace it is when we understand this and choose to build bridges, inviting others in rather than building walls to keep them out. Perhaps the Father knows what we do not: that there is healing and peace in unity, and to live in this connection means we must bear with one another, because others will certainly need to bear with us.

PRAY & BELIEVE

Father, I trust You, but I don't want to build bridges. I want to keep those who hurt me out of my life. You love unity, though, so I am willing to walk in Your ways, even in my weakness. I can't do it on my own, though. Help me. Give me a desire to love those who hurt me, be kind, and even pray for them. Heal the wounds they caused me so they are no longer remembered. Give me the strength to love them, forgive them, invite them into my life, and teach me how to have appropriate boundaries, so I stay safe. I do trust You, Father. Use this for Your glory and my growth. Amen.

PAUSE TO CONSIDER HIM

Who do you need to forgive? Are you willing to forgive them? Are you willing to ask the Lord to give you that desire? Sometimes we don't even want to ask for the desire! What does it mean to you, to build bridges?

_____
_____
_____
_____
_____
_____
_____

What are some actions you can take, small ones, to begin contraction on the bridge?

_____
_____
_____
_____
_____
_____

What is your take-away from this lesson?

_____
_____
_____
_____
_____
_____
_____

I Praise You For

-
-
-

The Gift of the Struggle

Count it all joy, my brothers, when you meet trials of various kinds, for you know that the testing of your faith produces steadfastness. And let steadfastness have its full effect, that you may be perfect and complete, lacking in nothing.

James 1:2-4

It seems outrageous to think that the struggles we face can be gifts. What kind of gift is a struggle? It doesn't seem very reasonable.

The Bible repeatedly says that God uses the things that seem foolish to confound or confuse the wise. But how so? How can we count difficulties as joy and struggles as gifts? Because the Lord operates in such ways: He knows deeper truths than we do, and His understanding is unsearchable. We must, therefore, *believe* His instructions before we will see its fruit.

This Scripture is just such an example. The world sees Believers as weak and needy. However, in trying times, the Believer who stands fast is the source of strength for the others shaking at their knees. Perhaps this strength is the gift.

Struggle does one of two things in a person's life: it makes them dig deep, hold fast, stand while the winds blow and the rain pelts, or give up, let go, and allow the winds to carry them away. This is why the Scripture says to count it joy; it is in the trials where we learn how to stand. It is in the heartache we gain spiritual muscles to hold fast. In the pain, the Believer can sleep in peace, knowing the Father is in charge, He will not fail, and we become steadfast.

Once we gain all the strength we can in a trial, we will have grown and become steadfast, withstanding the storm. That is the gift of the struggle.

PRAY & BELIEVE

Father, You know all things, and You know that I need You. Give me eyes to see those situations I'd rather avoid, as opportunities to grow. Teach me to trust You, even in trouble. Lord, I am the most needy of all Your children. I am not ashamed to admit that. Help me to run to You, in trials, not away from You. Call me, Lord, and let me hear Your voice when all I hear is noise. Be my joy in trial and peace. Teach me to remain steadfast regardless of my situation and use all things to draw me nearer to You. Amen,

PAUSE TO CONSIDER HIM

Is there any way you can see that your trials have been used to strengthen and grow you in faith? What trial are you facing now and how can you begin to be thankful IN (not for) the trial? Are you able to count your blessings in the midst of the trial?

_____
_____
_____
_____
_____
_____
_____
_____

How are you a better person today because of what you learned in past trials?

_____
_____
_____
_____
_____
_____
_____

What is your take-away from this lesson?

_____
_____
_____
_____
_____
_____
_____

I Praise You For

Forgiveness: A Path to Healing

*Be kind to one another, tenderhearted, forgiving
one another, as God in Christ forgave you.*

Ephesians 4:32

If we read this verse in its entirety before trying to dissect it to understand it fully, we will find two essential things: being kind and tenderhearted. While being put first in the sentence, it actually has a bit of a qualifier: forgiving one another.

If we are being instructed to forgive, it indicates something was done that requires forgiveness. And not only forgiving but also doing so with kindness and tenderheartedness. Christ forgave us for our sake so that we could receive eternal life in Heaven with Christ. But when we forgive, it is not for the other person but for ourselves. It frees us!

Unforgiveness is a heavy burden. It is time-consuming and exhausting. Keeping track of everyone's wrongdoings against us takes an emotional and physical toll. Unforgiveness turns to bitterness and can cause sicknesses such as headaches, neck strains, and even skin disorders. No wonder the Bible instructs us repeatedly to forgive others.

When we realize the depths of the Father's forgiveness toward us, His grace, and the price it cost to pay the debt we owed, how can we keep forgiveness from one who has hurt us?

Forgiving others brings healing. Perhaps the relationship is not entirely salvageable right away, but the mental act of forgiving allows us to be healed from the pain of remembering what was done to us. The memory may remain, but it will be just that—a memory. Forgiveness allows the emotional baggage that comes with the memory to end, bringing healing to our spirit, body, and soul.

PRAY & BELIEVE

Lord God, help me to put forgiveness into context. I know I have done many things that require forgiveness, and I always expect others to forgive me quickly and easily. But Father, I admit that I have trouble, often, forgiving others. Please give me the desire and courage to forgive those who've hurt me. Please help me understand that forgiving others while letting them off the hook for their actions frees me. Give me the courage to not hold a grudge, and to be kind and tender toward others, especially those who've hurt me. Amen.

PAUSE TO CONSIDER HIM

Who are you holding unforgiveness toward? Consider what you've required forgiveness for from others, and think about what the Lord has forgiven you for. Understanding this, can you find the strength to forgive others? How?

_____
_____
_____
_____
_____
_____
_____

How are you a better person today because of being forgiven?

_____
_____
_____
_____
_____
_____

What is your take-away from this lesson?

_____
_____
_____
_____
_____
_____

I Praise You For

-
-
-

Embracing Imperfection

But now, O Lord, you are our Father; we are the clay,
and you are our potter; we are all the work of your hand.

Isaiah 64:8

We strive for perfection. A friend of mine, a young man in his early thirties, has lived his entire life with the mindset of, "If I can't do it perfectly, I'm not going to do it at all." This is an unachievable goal.

The Bible instructs us that "whatever our hands find to do, to do that thing with all our hearts," but this doesn't imply perfection. Only one is perfect, and it absolutely is not us.

God is the creator, the perfect One. He molds, He shapes, He tweaks. I've watched as a crafted potter spins his wheel and dampens a blob of clay. As the wheel spins, that potter pulls the clay up and pushes it down. He forces it out to create a water pitcher, and just as I think, "Oh, he done—that's incredible!" he throws water onto it and, with his gifted hands, pushes it in, stretches it up, and turns it into a tall vase.

It is mesmerizing watching a skilled potter. I imagine that is the Father, as He shapes and molds and sees an imperfection somewhere down near the bottom, so he goes there and works that flaw out. There is something so embracing about pottery. Put a piece with its imperfections beside a stack of factory-made dishes, and one will automatically pick up the pottery. It has a different feel and a different look. It seems solid, sturdy, trustworthy even.

We are like that. God, the Master Potter, holds us in His capable hands. He takes great care in creating us into what He chooses. We will always have imperfections because there is none perfect but Him. But in His perfection, we can embrace and appreciate our flaws because we are fully assured that, flaws and all, He is not finished with us yet.

PRAY & BELIEVE

Master, You are the potter. You are crafted and skilled and know me— every flaw and crack. Yet, You love me anyway. Remind me that I am the clay, pliable, and moldable, and you can be trusted to keep me. I want to know you more. Teach my heart to see others as clay and not expect perfection from them. Let me see others as You do and love them, regardless of their actions. You are the potter of them as well, and You are molding them into beautiful vessels, but remind me that it takes time to trust You more. Amen.

PAUSE TO CONSIDER HIM

What do you think is your biggest character flaw or "crack"? Is it an area that the Lord is working in? Can you give it to Him and allow Him to do what a potter would do and reshape it? Are you ok if it remains a crack?

_____

_____

_____

_____

_____

_____

_____

What is an area that the Lord is currently highlighting that He wants to improve?

_____

_____

_____

_____

_____

_____

_____

What is your take-away from this lesson?

_____

_____

_____

_____

_____

_____

_____

I Praise You For

-
-
-

Grace for Every Scar

---

casting all your anxieties on him, because he cares for you.

1 Peter 5:7

Every scar tells a story. Sometimes, those stories are minor and dull; others tell of a life-harrowing journey. Some are visible on the flesh, and they heal far more quickly than the ones on the soul. Those wounds can take a lifetime to heal, leaving the biggest scars nobody will ever see.

It is these scars where God's grace shows up sufficiently. These ones can cause a person severe anxiety, few more painful than the ones printed on the heart of a child whose parents decide to call it quits. Children are delicate, yet we say they are resilient. They have to be, but their souls bear the wounds.

Maybe that child was you, and you continue to fight to heal those long-ago made wounds. You may wonder if they will ever heal, and just when you think they have, a situation will present itself and rip them right back open.

But God. God holds the healing balm, for He is the healer. He cares so deeply for His children, both young and old. He saw the soul as it was torn apart and sees it now as it struggles to forgive, to let go, and to internalize the truth that it really was not their fault.

As a grown man now, I was that child. I can attest to the absolute fact that the Father does heal the wounds, and He will close up those scars so beautifully that they will no longer seep out pain or memories, but instead, because He is so very good, they will serve a purpose. Maybe to better understand someone else's pain and keep you from making similar mistakes and maybe to teach you more about Christ.

Trust Him. Give Him your anxiety and pains, for He truly cares for you.

PRAY & BELIEVE

Lord, You know the wounds of my soul. You alone see them and understand them. I don't want to remember them anymore. I want You to remove them and heal those places damaged so long ago. There is shrapnel left that reminds me of the pain I felt as a little kid. Please dig the shrapnel out and touch all the places that still bleed. Father, I want to be healed. I want to be whole. I was not resilient then, and I'm not resilient now. But You were with me then, and You're with me today. Give me understanding, but more than that, please give me peace and joy. I trust You and love You. Thank you for never leaving me alone and for healing the broken places in my heart. Amen.

PAUSE TO CONSIDER HIM

Ask the Lord to show you where the shrapnel has stuck and then ask Him to dig it out. Are you ok with it hurting a little bit in order for it to be removed and healed? Ask the good Father to take the emotion from the memories and heal them entirely.

_____
_____
_____
_____
_____
_____
_____
_____

How do you see your life improving if the emotion is removed from your memories?

_____
_____
_____
_____
_____
_____

What is your take-away from this lesson?

_____
_____
_____
_____
_____
_____

I Praise You For

-
-
-

Creating a New Legacy

Therefore, if anyone is in Christ, he is a new creation.
The old has passed away; behold, the new has come.

2 Corinthians 5:17

What legacy do you dream about leaving for those you love? Wealth? Fame? This is the legacy the world strives to leave. But we are not of the world. Our legacy must reflect differently.

No matter your past, what was the legacy of those before you? It doesn't have to be yours. The Word says that if we are in Christ, we are entirely a new being. We have not been changed or modified, but brand new. Whatever was before you, your past, your experiences, they are gone. They do not define you.

Only Christ can cause such a newness to come. A friend recently saw this play out right in front of their eyes. Their story went like this:

"My grandmother passed away. She was gone. We did not sit and look at the casket, waiting for her to hop on out, because she had passed away. That very same day, my daughter had a baby. It was brand new. We beamed with joy at the sounds, smells, and sight of this new being. We snuggled her close and breathed her in. She was perfect and entirely without flaws. In one day, the old passed away, and the new had come."

While this story is in the flesh as a visual picture, the scripture refers to the soul. Once we are in Christ, the old soul dies: it can no longer remain and cannot return. It is not changed, fixed, or modified. It is dead. In its place is brand new: the Spirit of God Himself now lives within. We are brand new.

Let your legacy be one of the soul of a new man. Everywhere you go, leave grace, leave joy, leave the peace of God. What a legacy!

PRAY & BELIEVE

Lord, help me not to chase after things not of You. I desire to leave a legacy, be remembered after I'm gone, and have people speak of me in a particular way. But I give You my desires now and ask instead for Yours. What legacy do You want me to leave, Lord? Change me from the inside out, and teach me to walk not as a broken person wearing band-aids but as a brand new person. Open my eyes to let me see when I am returning to the old man, and have the courage to lay that one down and strive to live every day as the new person You have made me to be. Teach me, Lord, to walk in my new skin. Amen.

PAUSE TO CONSIDER HIM

If you coud create any legacy you wanted, what would it look like? Can you give that to the Father and trust Him to create in you the legacy He wants? Do you believe your experiences of the past define you?

_____
_____
_____
_____
_____
_____
_____
_____

How would your life be more peaceful if you let go of your desires and accepted His?

_____
_____
_____
_____
_____
_____
_____

What is your take-away from this lesson?

_____
_____
_____
_____
_____
_____
_____

I Praise You For

-
-
-

Faithful in the Fractures

The Lord is near to the brokenhearted and saves the crushed in spirit.

Psalm 34:18

Crushed in spirit. Those words alone can make a soul anguish, but if you've ever truly experienced that crushing, you know it is a pain that no words can explain and no tears can resolve.

Even as adults, we are not mentally equipped to deal efficiently with a broken heart or crushed spirit. These things do not describe the regular rejection or hurt we all experience throughout life; these hurts are so much deeper, and we humans are not equipped to understand or overcome such pain. God never intended for His children to experience this depth of heartache and soul-crushing pain.

Regardless, we do. Especially a child whose family is disintegrating right before their eyes, and they are powerless to do anything to stop it. The child, stable and happy only days ago, is now given the news that one parent is moving out. The child is assured it's not their fault, and that they will still see the other parent. The adults try desperately to ensure the children won't be affected, but they are. How can a child not be torn apart when the adults in their life are broken and hurting themselves?

But God knows. He sees beyond the smiling masks and brave faces everyone is wearing while trying to pretend they are ok. God understands that depth of pain. He moves in close, grabs you, and holds on tight: He may not remove the pain nor repair the relationships; He doesn't always fix the problems, but He will come near and hold you close. He will give strength as needed, and joy will, one day, stir again. In the midst of a broken heart, God is near. Just stop for a moment and breathe Him in; He will carry you even in the storm.

PRAY & BELIEVE

Father, I have spent days with a broken heart. I do know that crushing of the soul is where it looks like life will end. But it doesn't, and I know that You are near me, walking with me and holding me up when I can't stand on my own. When the rest of the world fails me, You never do. When others leave, You stay. I do know this because Your word says it's true. Help me believe it even when I cannot see it or when it feels like You are far away. I cannot walk this road alone. Be my strength when I am without any, and soften my heart to love others, even when I don't want to. I trust You to keep me. Amen.

PAUSE TO CONSIDER HIM

When you look back, can you see God in the fractures? Ask Him to show you how He was protecting you in those situations. Looking forward, can you trust that He is healing those same fractures to make you a stronger, more peace-filled person?

_____
_____
_____
_____
_____
_____
_____

How would your life improve if you let God heal the fractures and restore your soul?

_____
_____
_____
_____
_____
_____
_____

What is your take-away from this lesson?

_____
_____
_____
_____
_____
_____

I Praise You For

-
-
-

The God of Second Chances

The steadfast love of the Lord never ceases; his mercies never come to an end; they are new every morning; great is your faithfulness.

Lamentations 3:22-23

Who can understand such a thing as a continual, steadfast love? What does that mean, and how can we earn something phenomenally life-impacting? Humans are all about earning and keeping the love of those around us.

Maybe the home you were raised in wasn't filled with all-inclusive, unconditional love. Perhaps you felt you needed to perform, attain certain grades, or be the best on the sports team in order to be loved. So many of us were lied to by the enemy of our soul and not necessarily by our families that we were not loveable. Many of us carry that lie through life, but it's time to put that lie to rest.

If you have been one of those who, for one reason or another, grew up thinking you were not loved or had to earn the love of those around you, I have good news! That belief is misguided and an outright lie. You are loveable and worthy of receiving love. You get a second chance now and can move ahead knowing this great life-changing truth.

God Himself loves you with an everlasting love. His love for you is steadfast, all-consuming, never-ending, unearned, and undeserved. Before you knew Him, He knew and loved you.

People don't intentionally hurt our hearts, but people are frail. We are sinners, broken, often passing down what was passed down to us through the generations because that's what humans do. But God is not human. His love for you is perfect. Believe it is for you because it is. Receive the second chance He is offering.

PRAY & BELIEVE

Father, I have sometimes believed that I am not worthy of love and that love is something to be earned. In my life, I have learned the wrong concept of what love really is, and it has caused me to make some bad choices that have left me with undesired consequences. Would You, Father, teach me the truth about love? Plant in my heart the truth that I don't need to earn Your love or work to keep it. You will never remove it from me; I cannot lose it. Heal up the cracks in my heart caused by those I loved who were supposed to love me. Help me remember they were broken, and it wasn't my fault. Confirm in my heart that I am loveable, accepted, and worthy of love. Amen.

PAUSE TO CONSIDER HIM

Do you see yourself as worthy of love? Ask the Father to show you how deep His love is. Consider that His love for you is without conditions. He will never withdraw from you and you can never be out of His sight. What does that truth do to you heart?

_____
_____
_____
_____
_____
_____
_____

If you could grasp fully the truth of God's love, how would that change you?

_____
_____
_____
_____
_____
_____

What is your take-away from this lesson?

_____
_____
_____
_____
_____
_____
_____

I Praise You For

-
-
-

Becoming Who You Were Meant to Be

And I am sure of this, that he who began a good work in you
will bring it to completion at the day of Jesus Christ.

Philippians 1:6

This Scripture is often quoted but rarely pondered. There are layers to this Scripture, and it would serve us well to take some time to pause and think about some of the good works the Lord has started in us so that we might have a persevering hope for our future.

God created us with a purpose. We are not here just to take up space and pass the time. God is purposeful in all He does, and the Scripture references that there is a book on each of our lives in the library of Heaven. We don't know what is written in our books, but He knows. He wrote them, and He will empower us to become who He created us to be.

If the Creator has written the book on our lives, then He is fully capable of bringing those thing to be in our lives. But we have a role to play: to be diligent, to walk humbly, to fashion our lives after His Word and His instruction, and to spend time with Him to gain wisdom, understanding, and direction.

It is He who started the work and He who will finish the work. He called us from darkness to do good works in light before we ever existed. And, once we have completed the things He set out for us to accomplish, we will move to our eternal home to spend eternity with the author of our stories.

He sees the struggles we face and turns our pain into victory, using what the enemy meant for evil into good for God's glory. Do not give up. Your story is not over. God is transforming your story into something amazing that He can use for your good and His glory.

PRAY & BELIEVE

Lord God, You know my life from beginning to end. You know my thoughts, my hopes, and my desires. You see where I have failed miserably, and You can take those failings and turn them into blessings. You know my story. You planned good works for me and will direct and guide me into those very things. When I get frustrated or impatient, remind me that You are steering the ship. Keep me from quitting what You have begun in my life, and show me what things are not in my story so I can let them go. I don't want to waste my days on things You have not planned for me. You know my desires, but I would rather have Your plans than mine. Amen.

PAUSE TO CONSIDER HIM

What work do you think God started in you? Do you think He has changed His mind? Is He capable of causing all things to work together for you, so that His plan for you can work out? Can you trust Him to work things out in your favor?

_____
_____
_____
_____
_____
_____
_____
_____

How would your life look differently if you believed, fully, that He is for you?

_____
_____
_____
_____
_____
_____
_____
_____

What is your take-away from this lesson?

_____
_____
_____
_____
_____
_____
_____

I Praise You For

When Home Hurts

Peace I leave with you; my peace I give to you. Not as the world gives do I give to you. Let not your hearts be troubled, neither let them be afraid.

John 14:27

We all want peace: peace in our homes, in our souls, in our relationships, and our world. Unfortunately, we often have so much that fights against us that peace seems to be non-existent most days.

If you grew up in a home where there was yelling or fighting, slamming doors, and parents deciding to go their own way, you know the pain and fear that comes from this lack of earthly peace. Sometimes, the place that was supposed to be our safe place was the very place that was unsafe. Maybe you experienced the fact that the people who were supposed to protect and love you were the ones who were too busy fighting their own demons to do so. Sometimes, home hurts.

But God can be trusted. He will never be too busy or too distant to see you. He gives peace, unmeasured, always. But the peace God offers is not of this world. It doesn't have the same outer shell we look for because it is an inner peace that is unseen but experienced deeper than any peace the world can offer.

Even in crises, our souls can be at peace. In the midst of chaos, our hearts can be at rest. How is this so? Because God's peace is in God. It is in a faithful knowledge of who He is and what He offers. The peace God offers is independent of the world, unaffected by circumstances, unable to be disrupted or extinguished.

If you look back at childhood with regret, look up. If your home was a source of pain, look up. Give it to God, and let Him use a painful past to create a hopeful present. Accept the peace He offers, the peace that the world can never take away. Just look up.

PRAY & BELIEVE

Father God, I would love for the peace the world gives, but I need the peace of You. You are never too busy or far away where I cannot find You. You provide the peace that really matters. Lord, help me to trust You deeper, where my heart does not waver and my hope doesn't fade. You never fail. God, but sometimes my heart is so troubled, even though I struggle for it not to be, that I waver and get worried. I cannot find peace without You. Heal my heart and cause my emotions not to rule me anymore. Keep my heart from being troubled, Lord, and take my fear. I don't want it. Amen.

PAUSE TO CONSIDER HIM

What does peace look like to you? How would you describe a peaceful future? Can you believe that peace is something different than what the world teaches? Ask the Lord to bring the peace that is beyond understanding, into your heart and mind.

_____
_____
_____
_____
_____
_____
_____
_____

How would your life be changed if you had peace in your soul and mind?

_____
_____
_____
_____
_____
_____

What is your take-away from this lesson?

_____
_____
_____
_____
_____
_____

I Praise You For

-
-
-

The Beauty of a Scar

And we know that for those who love God all things work together for good, for those who are called according to his purpose.

Romans 8:28

Every scar tells a story. That is the beauty of a scar: the story that's behind it. Some stories are quite insignificant, without emotional attachment, and barely worth recalling. But others are life-changing, and those ones, well, they are the ones we retell over and over because they changed us and not necessarily for the better—yet. But over time, as the wounds heal, those scars become a thing of beauty because they come to represent growth.

The most significant are often the scars left on our souls. Feeling abandoned or unwanted etch deep wounds that leave us wondering if we are even loveable. If those who were supposed to protect and care for us fail to do so, the wounds cut deep, and the healing is long and painful.

But God is faithful. He never abandons His own and assures those who are His that He works all things together for good—eventually.

It might seem that God is slow in keeping His Word, but He isn't. It might feel that He has left us alone, but He hasn't. Circumstances may appear like He's not for us, but He is. As we mature, we learn not to judge God based on our feelings but rather on His Word. We must agree with God, knowing He can be trusted to take our scars and turn them into beauty.

Jesus bore the scars of a cross, of complete abandonment, of absolute rejection; yet, those are the most beautiful scars in all of history—and in all that is yet to come.

PRAY & BELIEVE

You, Lord, bear the scars that tell the greatest story of all time. Oh, how Your heart must have broken when the Father turned away from You because of my sin. Thank you for bearing my burden and paying the price for my sin. When my life seems to be a disaster, remind me that You work all these things together for good. You will not let me go because You paid the biggest price for me, and You are good. Amen.

PAUSE TO CONSIDER HIM

Think about the biggest scar in your life. What was the story behind it? Have you found healing from the pain of the wound? Do you want healing? Ask the Lord to take the emotion from that wound, leaving just a scar, then trust Him to do it.

_____
_____
_____
_____
_____
_____
_____

How would your life look differently if the scar stopped bleeding and the pain ended?
_____
_____
_____
_____
_____
_____

What is your take-away from this lesson?
_____
_____
_____
_____
_____
_____
_____

I Praise You For

-
-
-

Embracing Change

Behold, I am doing a new thing; now it springs forth, do you not perceive it? I will make a way in the wilderness and rivers in the desert.

Isaiah 43:19

Change is hard. Getting stuck in a rut is easy. Being comfortable in our world is the easiest rut to fall into and the most difficult to give up when required. Humans are obsessed with personal comfort. There is nothing wrong with our desire to live every day in comfort, but it is essential to understand that God is not all that concerned with our level of comfort. We know this to be true for a couple of reasons.

First, the Bible tells us so. He never strove for it personally, and while His disciples certainly wanted to live in daily comfort, Jesus never led them that way. No Bible character, in fact, lived a life of comfort, and we should expect the same: to spend much time being uncomfortable.

While God never promises that we will live in comfort in this life, He does promise ways through difficult times. When He says He will make a way through the wilderness, we can believe that we will spend at least some of our time in the desert. When He says He will supply rivers in the desert, we must trust that deserts will be a part of our journey.

Life is all about change. Each year brings so many changes, some good others not, but we cannot avoid them. We do not have the foresight to see potholes, whereby missing them, but God does. He is the leader, and we get to follow. He is the the Provider, we are the needer. He is the giver, we are the beggar.

While humans don't like change, we can trust that God is doing new things, making ways, and using all things for our good and His glory. Embrace change and trust God. He has gone before you, and He will make a way.

PRAY & BELIEVE

Lord, help me to be less concerned with my comfort level and more concerned with those around me. Grow me up into who You want me to be. I know You don't need me, but You want me. Thank you for choosing me to belong to You and for opening my ears to hear Your voice. I am in such need, but I know You are the Provider who sees all my needs and will meet every one of them in Your timing and ways. Help me to be patient and keep my hope in You. Amen.

PAUSE TO CONSIDER HIM

On a scale of one to ten, how important is personal comfort to you? What does that look like? Would you be ok if some of those comforts were taken from you? Can you adjust what comfort looks like? Ask the Lord to show you His idea of comfort for you.

_____
_____
_____
_____
_____
_____
_____

How would your life change if you adopted His idea of comfort, giving up your own?

_____
_____
_____
_____
_____
_____

What is your take-away from this lesson?

_____
_____
_____
_____
_____
_____

I Praise You For

-
-
-

No Longer Weary

Come to me, all who labor and are heavy laden, and I will give
you rest. Take my yoke upon you, and learn from me, for I am
gentle and lowly in heart, and you will find rest for your souls.
For my yoke is easy, and my burden is light.

Matthew 11:28-30

Who among us is not weary these days? It seems that no matter who is asked the question, *How are you*? The answer is the same: *Tired. I am tired.* This is not the kind of tired that a nap, or sleeping in a few extra minutes will fix. This is the worn-out and weary kind of tired. We are weary. The world wears us down over time. But we do not have to continue to drag that heaviness with us.

Sometimes, we are laden (which simply means to carry a heavy load) with present circumstances: illness, lack of funds, loneliness, or the stresses of life. Other times, our heavy load is from things past: guilt of past choices, baggage from past relationships, or residual pain from childhood trauma. Whether past memories or present circumstances, being heavy-laden makes us tired and weary. It feels like we've been dragging a suitcase filled with bricks and are worn out.

But we can rise from the ashes and step out of the ruins of our past baggage. We can come to God, the Healer of our souls, and give Him the suitcase. He wants to dispose of it! He says, "Come here, child. Why are you still dragging that suitcase? Those are not your bricks, and that is not your suitcase. It's too heavy for you, child. It's wearing you out." And He is holding out His hand to take it, but you must be willing to hand it over.

He has a trade for you: the bricks for peace—the suitcase for rest. Let the past go, trust Him in the present, and hope in Him for a future.

PRAY & BELIEVE

God, I am tired. This world is a tough place to be and there seems to be very little reprieve. But You promise to give me rest. I need that rest that You provide; the rest that relieves my mind and calms my fears. Sometimes, memories wear me down; sometimes, it's shrapnel from a past I could not control. But You know, Lord. You see when I come unraveled, I don't feel like I can hang on. Grab ahold of me, and please don't let me go. I trust You, but give me the ability to trust You more. Give me rest, Lord, so I am no longer weary. Amen.

PAUSE TO CONSIDER HIM

Are you heavy laden? Do you see yourself as a victim? Ask the Lord to give you the courage to exchange that victim mindset to one of victory. Choosing to not be a victim does not mean bad things didn't happen to you, it only means you rose above them.

_____
_____
_____
_____
_____
_____
_____

How would your life change if you could walk in victory instead of victimhood?

_____
_____
_____
_____
_____
_____

What is your take-away from this lesson?

_____
_____
_____
_____
_____
_____

I Praise You For

-
-
-

The Promise of Restoration

*Brothers, I do not consider that I have made it my own. But
one thing I do: forgetting what lies behind and straining
forward to what lies ahead, I press on toward the goal for the
prize of the upward call of God in Christ Jesus.*

Philippians 3:13-14

If you have ever restored something, you'll know there's an essential step one must take before the restoration can occur. Whether it's a '62 Corvette, an old house, or a human soul, if the step of preparation is not thoroughly completed, the restoration will be temporary.

When restoring a car, there is sanding of the rust and ripping out the torn leather. In a home, restoration begins with demolition, and when a promise of restoring the soul is made, there is a forgetting of the past that must take place.

One cannot hold onto the past while trying to walk in the present. The past is like a chain, keeping you bound. It must be let go, forgotten, and forgiven if one is to enjoy the promise of a glorious present and future.

This is an ongoing process. Pressing on, as Paul puts it, is hard work. He uses the word *Straining*, indicating it's no easy, one-and-done thing. We do the *Straining*, God does the restoring. We do the *Pressing On*, and He provides the prize.

For us to experience a lasting restoration that will give us the power to press on, we must forget the past and walk out of the chains that have bound us to it.

Let God restore all the wounded pieces in your soul and then leave them in the past. Press forward in the call God has for you.

PRAY & BELIEVE

Father, restore me. I know it's a little-by-little process, so surround me with patience. I know I cannot press forward without letting go of the past. It's hard, Lord. I want to let it go, but I want to hold onto it. There is a certain victim power in holding onto past pain. Show me how to let it all go and give me the desire to do so. Open my eyes to see the prize that You have set before me, and keep it in the forefront of my mind. I need a great tenacity to keep pressing on when I want to give up. Chisel the rough edges from me so the restoration can be complete and thorough. Amen.

PAUSE TO CONSIDER HIM

Have you ever restored anything? What was that experience like? Can you see how it is similar to God restoring a human heart? Ask the Lord to restore your heart, chiseling away all the old, rough areas and replacing them with the oil of joy.

_____
_____
_____
_____
_____
_____
_____
_____

What would your life look like if you had a restored heart and mind?

_____
_____
_____
_____
_____
_____
_____

What is your take-away from this lesson?

_____
_____
_____
_____
_____
_____
_____

I Praise You For

-
-
-

Faith in the Storm

And he awoke and rebuked the wind and said to the sea, "Peace! Be still!" And the wind ceased, and there was a great calm.

Mark 4:39

The Bible never promised that once we followed Christ, the winds and waves and storms of life would cease. We were never told the pain from the past, or burdens from our present would disappear. We know that storms will still come, but it's not the storm where we need to focus our attention, but in the One who has power over them.

Even the disciples who walked physically with Christ every day, who knew Him personally as a friend, were afraid. They were also shocked when the wind and the waves obeyed Jesus. They replied, "We believe, but help our unbelief!" If the disciples, who personally saw miracle after miracle from their friend, were surprised at His power over even the storm on the sea, how much more should we trust that He will calm the storms in our own lives?

We cannot avoid storms. Oh yes, sometimes our choices add to the storm, and other times, trying to avoid it makes the storm that much worse. But storms are a thing of life. How satisfying to know the One who has the power to utter the words, "Peace, Be Still."

God is our anchor in the storm. Sometimes He calms it, and other times, He allows the winds to batter us because He knows that is when roots grow deep. We run to Him in a storm. We fall to our knees when the wind bashes against us. This is where we find Him, where we grow, where our faith is built, and where we learn more about who He is.

Don't fear the storms. Instead, have faith in the midst of them, knowing you are not alone: God is in the boat, and He will, in due time, speak the words, "Peace. Be Still," and you will come out stronger, knowing Him.

PRAY & BELIEVE

Lord, some days, my life feels like I'm smack in the middle of a storm. It seems like the winds of fear or the waves of doubt rage around me, and I do not have the power to stop any of it. But You can calm everything that rages around me. You can, with a word, direct it all to cease. At the same time, You can empower me with the strength to stand in the middle, knowing You are my anchor. I would desire that You command all that rages to stop. But if not, fill my heart with resilience to stand in the middle without wavering, knowing You are my anchor even in the middle of all that burdens me. Thank you. Amen.

PAUSE TO CONSIDER HIM

Are you in a storm right now? What is causing you fear or doubt? If not now, what storm have you faced in the past where it seemed too heavy and you felt powerless to stop what was happening and had no ability of your own to withstand it?

_____
_____
_____
_____
_____
_____
_____

How are you a better person today because of what you learned in that experience?

_____
_____
_____
_____
_____
_____

What is your take-away from this lesson?

_____
_____
_____
_____
_____
_____

I Praise You For

The Goodness of God in Every Season

For the Lord is good; his steadfast love endures forever,
and his faithfulness to all generations.

Psalm 100:5

Recently, a friend received some excellent news. He had been praying for his house to sell for the asking price, and when it did, the shouts went up, "Oh, God is good, brother!" He is good. That is not up for debate. But I wondered if he would have been just as convinced of God's goodness if the house hadn't sold for weeks—months even.

We all do the same. When things work out as we'd hoped and prayed, our first response is, "God is good." When situations arise that are less exciting and even troublesome, we rarely respond with the same fervor of God's goodness. But He is equally good in every situation.

Wrongly, we believe that when things go how we desire, that is the best thing. But our desires are often self-motivated, leaving no room for growth. A man goes to the gym to build strength. It's hard work, usually painful, and resistance builds the muscle. Never do we think, "Those weights are terrible, how they are so heavy." We WANT heavier weights; even though we know they will cause our muscles to hurt, we also know that we will become stronger through that pain.

God is like those weights. He allows or causes resistance, at times, for our growth. He desires us to be strong in the power of Him. Strength is built not in good times but in hardship. Our Father is like the spotter, right beside us with His arms extended; for that exact second, we need help. He says, "You can do this ... I am right here with you ... I won't let you fall." This is the goodness of God.

God is good; full stop. In hardship and pain, or joy and peace, He is good.

PRAY & BELIEVE

God, I know that You are always good. I believe in my head that You are good whether things go my way or not, but I need You to help me move that knowledge to my heart so I do not doubt in challenging times. You know how I desire things to go, but You know better, and I trust You to do what is best for me. Help me, even when it looks like things are not going in my favor, that You are good, and in the end, it will work out for my best, my growth, my strength, and the building of my faith. Remind me every day that You are good. Full Stop. Amen.

PAUSE TO CONSIDER HIM

Think back to a moment in life when you didn't see how you'd make it through, but now you can see that God was doing what was the best and in the end, you could see His goodness. Pause and consider how you grew because of it:

_____
_____
_____
_____
_____
_____
_____

How are you a better person today because of what you learned in that experience?

_____
_____
_____
_____
_____
_____

What is your take-away from this lesson?

_____
_____
_____
_____
_____
_____

I Praise You For

-
-
-

Hope Amidst the Trials

---

not only that, but we rejoice in our sufferings, knowing that
suffering produces endurance, and endurance produces
character, and character produces hope,

Romans 5:3-4

No human on this earth, past, current, or present, looks forward to trouble. We don't get excited about it, and instead work hard to avoid it. Regardless, trouble comes. It finds us from time to time throughout life, and we can do nothing to stop it. As sure as the sun will rise in the morning, trouble will find us periodically in this world.

The good news is that God is aware and gives us a clear explanation of the results of such trouble. Many confuse this scripture and wrongly believe it suggests we be thankful FOR our sufferings, but this is not so. God does not expect us to be thankful for cancer, loss, heartbreak, rejection, death, or divorce of our parents.

The word is, instead, IN our sufferings. There is a world of difference here, and this is why we can have hope in the middle of the trials. We are to praise the Lord on good days and stormy nights. He desires our praise in the valley and on the mountain. So, if this is when we are to praise, then the circumstances of suffering should not determine whether or not we are praising the Lord.

The Word explains why we can rejoice, regardless of circumstance: because we know there is a reason—it is for our good that will benefit us on the other side. Suffering produces endurance, which leads to character, and finally, hope. If hope is found at the end, that is a reason to rejoice! No matter what your circumstance today, God is with you. He walks with you through the circumstance so you can rejoice, knowing that on the other side, you will find hope.

PRAY & BELIEVE

God, I honestly do not want to praise in suffering. I don't want to suffer at all. But Your word does not sugarcoat this world and does tell me I will face suffering as long as I am in this world. Help me. Give me a genuine desire to rejoice and praise You always, even in the middle of suffering. Remind me that it is not without its benefits and that it is in the middle of suffering where I can run to You, and You will be found every time. Show me where I have grown in the past, in the middle of trials, so that I will behave better next time. Amen.

PAUSE TO CONSIDER HIM

Are there areas in your life today where you feel as though you are suffering? Can you see that perhaps, God might have a purpose in allowing such things? Tell Him your woes, ask Him for relief from it, and then begin to praise Him IN the situation.

_____
_____
_____
_____
_____
_____
_____

How would your life look different if you could see suffering as an opportunity?

_____
_____
_____
_____
_____
_____

What is your take-away from this lesson?

_____
_____
_____
_____
_____
_____

I Praise You For

-
-
-

The Depths of His Affection

For I am sure that neither death nor life, nor angels nor rulers, nor things present nor things to come, nor powers, nor height nor depth, nor anything else in all creation, will be able to separate us from the love of God in Christ Jesus our Lord

Romans 8:38-39

Nothing in our past has the power to separate us from the love of God. We cannot earn it, nor do we deserve it. His love is not for sale; it cannot be bought or worked for, and it cannot be lost.

In this world, we have no understanding of such love because we have not experienced it. None of us have. No matter what kind of family you were raised in, this love was not present because only the King of Kings can promise—and carry out—this depth of affection.

Think of it like this: if you are married, there is no possible way you can be with your spouse at all times. Each of you does things in a day that cause you to have to be apart—be separated. If you have children, it's the same. They must go to school, and you are not allowed in the classroom all day, every day, so you cannot be ever-present with your child. There are times in the day when they will be separated from you. This does not mean you don't love them; you are simply not with them.

If something happens and you are needed, you must leave what you are doing and go to them. If you are with one child and another calls you, you say, "I'll be right back," and leave that one for a brief time. Many things will separate us from those we love at one time or another.

But God is never separated from us. He is with us always. Nothing, not death, angels, or powers of any kind, can separate us from the Master. When we need Him, He is there. When we are afraid, He is there. What a comfort to know we can never be separated from Him.

PRAY & BELIEVE

Lord, I do not have the ability as a human to understand this kind of love, but I do know that I am thankful for it. Open my understanding so I can know it and not doubt that You are with me every moment and that I am never out of Your sight. Lord, You are so good to me, and I do not deserve it. Thank you for Your love for me, not because of me but because of You. Thank you that Your love is without measure or conditions. Thank you that I do not earn it; therefore I cannot lose it. Remind me when I am afraid, overwhelmed, or anxious that You are with me, and I am forever safe in the shadow of Your wings. Amen.

PAUSE TO CONSIDER HIM

Think about how many times you do something to gain the kindness, love or respect of another person. Who, in your life, loves you without expectation or condition? God does. Can you plant that truth in your soul? How might that change how you see God?

_____
_____
_____
_____
_____
_____
_____

How does knowing this about God change you? How should it change you?

_____
_____
_____
_____
_____
_____
_____

What is your take-away from this lesson?

_____
_____
_____
_____
_____
_____

I Praise You For

-
-
-

Rooted in His Love

---

so that Christ may dwell in your hearts through faith—that you,
being rooted and grounded in love, may have strength to comprehend
with all the saints what is the breadth and length and height and
depth, and to know the love of Christ that surpasses knowledge, that
you may be filled with all the fullness of God.

Ephesians 3:17-19

I am convinced that we humans are incapable of fully understanding the love of Christ. It is beyond our limited comprehension; this phrase is overwhelming: *have the strength to comprehend.*

Have you ever considered that it takes strength to comprehend His love for you? Then, the following phrase makes sense. Understanding the unlimited love of a Savior, for us, takes strength. It has no top, no bottom, no sides. It stretches higher than the highest highs and lower than the lowest lows. It is beyond knowledge. Even thinking of it as these words are written overwhelms me.

What love has Christ for us? Now, all we can do is stop and ponder an unanswerable question. Pause and ponder it.

Now imagine how our lives would be different if we could somehow internalize this truth and live from the center of it. I imagine it to be like a well that is always bubbling with cool, clear water. God has said, "Go ahead, drink from it anytime you want. No matter how much you drink, the water will never be reduced. The more you drink, the more it produces."

Now, be rooted in that. Allow that love to overwhelm you, but then let it be the foundation from which you live, act, hope, and think. It changes a person. This love cannot leave one where they used to be, which I suppose, is the whole point of being rooted in His love.

PRAY & BELIEVE

Father God, how different my life might be if I could somehow understand and internalize Your love for me. I need to be rooted in that love. I want to be overwhelmed by it and live from it. Father, it's hard for a human to understand a love that does not exist in humanity, but if I could, it would change how I act, respond, and think. Lord, please help my limited mind understand such an unlimited love and teach me how to live from it. Thank you for loving me from that place, from which there are no limits. Amen.

PAUSE TO CONSIDER HIM

Have you ever considered that we need God's help to allow understanding of how deep His love for us is? Do you realize the fullness of such a love? Ask the Lord to open your understanding, and help you to understand the fullness of His love for you.

_____
_____
_____
_____
_____
_____
_____

How would your life look different if you understood the fulness of His love for you?

_____
_____
_____
_____
_____
_____

What is your take-away from this lesson?

_____
_____
_____
_____
_____
_____

I Praise You For

-
-
-

Everlasting Embrace

---

the Lord appeared to him from far away. I have loved you with an
everlasting love; therefore I have continued my faithfulness to you.

Jeremiah 31:3

Before you knew Him, He knew you. His eye has never diverted from your face. He sees your heart, bears your burden, hears your soul, and knows your thoughts. The Master of the universe has a detailed design for your life. Before you took a breath, He had planned for your days.

It's a hard truth to believe sometimes because life can have hard days, and we wonder why. But God knows even the hard days are for our growth. It is on the hard days that we run to Him and fall into His arms. When we can find no answers, no reason for our pain, we run to Him.

Far too often, when we find ourselves in the midst of a crisis or are the recipient of the pain from someone else's choices, we run away from God. We tend to blame Him because we need someone to blame. We can become angry with Him. That's ok. He knows. He understands the human heart and knows that, as humans, we can sometimes lash out at the ones who are not responsible for our hurt. He does not turn His back but instead keeps His face turned toward us and opens His arms to us.

He is a safe place to fall when our circumstances are against us. Run TO Him. He will catch you. He is waiting to comfort you and dry your tears. He will mend your heart and heal your soul. You will become stronger and come to understand He is faithful. He can be trusted, even with our brokenness.

He, too, was broken by the choices of others, but still, He loved because His love is everlasting and His faithfulness can be trusted.

PRAY & BELIEVE

Lord, I am sorry that I run away and hide so many times before coming to find You. Sometimes, I am like a child, hiding from the One who can help me! Father, forgive me for that, and as I grow in You, give me the courage to run to You and find peace and shelter in Your arms. Remind me that You are not angry with me; you do not want to punish me for every little thing. I can come to You and find rest, safety, and assurance that everything will be ok. I know You wait for me to come to You, so when I am tempted to run, call me to You and give me the courage to come unashamed. Amen.

PAUSE TO CONSIDER HIM

Think back to some situations where you ran from God instead of to Him. Did it help? How long did it take before you picked yourself up and went to Him? Did He turn His back or embrace You? What would it take for you to run to Him next time?

_____
_____
_____
_____
_____
_____
_____

How do you experience God, when you are facing a crisis?

_____
_____
_____
_____
_____
_____
_____

What is your take-away from this lesson?

_____
_____
_____
_____
_____
_____
_____

I Praise You For

Growth from Grief

Blessed be the God and Father of our Lord Jesus Christ, the Father of mercies and God of all comfort, who comforts us in all our affliction, so that we may be able to comfort those who are in any affliction, with the comfort with which we ourselves are comforted by God.

2 Corinthians 1:3-4

Why do we face afflictions? Why can't life be smooth sailing? We wonder such things and try our best to avoid any trouble that threatens to bother us, questioning the Lord when trouble comes our way. *Why, why, why?* We demand to know, as though knowing why would somehow make things easier or more acceptable.

But why is this our response to affliction? Why do we think our lives should be problem-free? If Jesus' life was filled with trouble and affliction, why would we think ours should not be? He knew the Father, as He came from Him. We know the Father because we know the Son. Even still, this doesn't seem to bring us comfort in the middle of affliction.

The worst affliction, possibly, is that over which we have no control. Families separating, people leaving, or not following through on a promise are all hurts that are out of our hands. But don't fail to see the hurt in these people's hearts. Don't forget that perhaps they are trying to heal their own pain and don't necessarily have the ability to notice the shrapnel their choices are leaving in the hearts of others.

Run to God for comfort, gain strength from Him, and once comforted, you are equipped to comfort others. What if we considered affliction an opportunity for growth and to know the Father deeper rather than a curse that we work hard to avoid? What if grief is for our growth?

God knows all we will face and has already come to the rescue. Move toward Him. He is waiting.

PRAY & BELIEVE

Lord, I do want to know why. Why me? Why couldn't my family just be perfect? Why did I have to endure the heartache? I know the answers, Lord. I know we live in a broken world, and people are broken. Sometimes, in one's striving for happiness, someone else gets hurt. I know, too, Father, that sometimes staying in certain situations is unsafe. But understanding why doesn't help the sadness. So, Father, I give all of it to You. Bless my family, and draw near them. Call out to them so they can run to you. Lord, forgive me for my demands of *Why* and help me use my experiences to comfort others. Amen.

PAUSE TO CONSIDER HIM

How can I use what I learned from my own circumstances to comfort others? Who do I know that might need comforting? How can I ensure that I do not follow in the same patterns as those before me? Can I let go of wanting to know why?

_____
_____
_____
_____
_____
_____
_____

How are you a better person today because of what you learned in that experience?

_____
_____
_____
_____
_____
_____

What is your take-away from this lesson?

_____
_____
_____
_____
_____
_____

I Praise You For

-
-
-

Abiding in the Vine

I am the vine; you are the branches. Whoever abides in me and I in him, he it is that bears much fruit, for apart from me you can do nothing.

John 15:5

Have you ever noticed a vineyard? They are stunning. From afar, they are often enormous and intriguing. But from up close, if you were to walk through one, it is something else. The smell is fresh and pure, filled with the sweetness of the fruit and the dirt from the earth. If you were to pluck off a handful of those berries at peak season, they would literally dance on your tongue.

The flavor would leave you wanting more. If one of those branches gets too heavy and falls to the dirt, the caretaker would not allow it to be trampled but instead carefully pick it up, clean it off, and weave it back into the vine so the fruit would not be wasted.

No branch has ever said to the vine, "I don't need you. I can grow this fruit myself. I have everything I need so I do not have any need for you." How ludicrous. It doesn't take a genius to know what would happen to that fruit: guaranteed death. But we do that repeatedly to the One who created us to abide in Him.

If we want to have fruit in our lives and walk in the fruit of the Spirit: love, joy, peace, patience, kindness, goodness, faithfulness, gentleness, and self-control, we must stay rooted in the vine. It is clear that if we do not stay connected, our fruit will be trampled and die.

Just as the vinedresser tends to and cares for the fruit of his vine, God tenderly cares for the branches that are part of His vine. Remember, we are not the vine but are connected to it. Everything we need comes from the vine, who is Christ. Don't try this life without Him; you won't make it. Stay close and connected and abide in the vine.

PRAY & BELIEVE

Father God, You are such a good Vine. You provide all I need, and even still, I often want to run from You. But keep me close, Lord. I desire to walk in the fruit of the Vine: love, joy, peace, patience, self-control, faithfulness, goodness. What a wonderful life it would be if everyone produced such fruit. I cannot control what others do or what kind of fruit they produce, but I can choose to abide in You and bear this fruit. When I am tempted to disengage from You and do my own thing, remind me of the fruit. Cause me to consider what kind of fruit I want to produce, and then give me the desire and tenacity to stay rooted in You. Amen.

PAUSE TO CONSIDER HIM

Think of a time when you were producing good fruit. Were you close to the Vine? Remember that the fruit we produce does not mean life will be without issue, but instead the good fruit will provide sustanance to endure through the hard times.

_____
_____
_____
_____
_____
_____
_____
_____

Make a plan to help you stay rooted in the Vine.

_____
_____
_____
_____
_____
_____

What is your take-away from this lesson?

_____
_____
_____
_____
_____
_____

I Praise You For

-
-
-

This is Not the End

Why are you cast down, O my soul, and why are you in turmoil within me? Hope in God; for I shall again praise him, my salvation and my God.

Psalm 42:11

When you think you are alone in your suffering, remember David. He was called to be a king, not only a king, but the greatest king Israel ever had or would have. How can we possibly relate to such a man? The answer is in the question: he was a man. He had no special superpowers, as one might think, but he was a mere mortal with pain and sorrow, fear and anxiety, just like us.

But David faced outrageous difficulties. He was a future king, stuck in the life of a shepherd. He was chased after, wanted dead, hiding in caves. He must have had thoughts racing in his mind, but rather than give in and give up, he reminded his soul to praise the Lord. Wow!

If we understand the soul's makeup, which includes our mind, will, and emotions, it makes sense that our words have an impact. Thoughts of the mind can strengthen the will, which drives emotion. They work together, yet separately. The beauty of this verse is that it reminds us of our control over the soul. As David reminded his soul that it was not the end for him but that God had plans and a future for his life, we can do the same.

When you are down, tell your soul to get up and praise the Lord. When life seems to be getting the best of you, remind your soul that God is still on the throne, He is in control, and He will not fail or forget you. Stand tall when the world seems to be crashing around you, and remind your soul that this is not the end. Get up and praise the Lord. Hope again in the Lord, set your eyes on Him, and know His eyes are still on you.

PRAY & BELIEVE

I want to be like David. Lord, teach me as You taught David. When his soul was downcast, he scolded it. Remind me, in moments of disappointment or when my soul is downcast, to get up and praise You. Evil cannot win when I praise You. Feelings cannot stay down when I praise You. Empower me to control my thoughts so my soul and emotions will get in line. I desire this kind of control over my life, but without You, it is impossible. Stay with me, Father, and remind me that You are still good, and I am still the apple of Your eye. I choose to set my hope on You again today and keep it there. Amen.

PAUSE TO CONSIDER HIM

Have you ever spoken to your soul? Does it seem strange to do such a thing? Are you willing to give it a try? Can you envision your soul as separate from you that you would talk to like a friend? If you knew your soul would listen, what would you say?

_____
_____
_____
_____
_____
_____
_____

Try speaking to your soul and record how you felt and what you noticed.

_____
_____
_____
_____
_____
_____

What is your take-away from this lesson?

_____
_____
_____
_____
_____
_____

I Praise You For

He is Faithful

He who calls you is faithful; he will surely do it.

1 Thessalonians 5:24

In order to believe that God is faithful, we must grasp two things tightly: an understanding of who He is and faith that He is who He says He is. Trusting God can, at least for me and I am sure for you, be like a pendulum. One minute, I trust him fully, and even a shadow of doubt can't be found. But the next, my heart is fluttering, my mind is racing, and I am begging Him to show up.

Often, I feel poorly for fluctuating like this, but then I remember that even the disciples on the boat had cracks in their lives where doubt crept in. In that moment, God did not condemn them but drew them in to trust Him more. I find the disciples' response encouraging in my moments of doubt: "Lord, we believe—but help our unbelief."

Those words used to confuse me, but as I get older, they confuse me less. We have areas in our lives where we know that we know He is faithful. In times where we have seen His hand repeatedly, it is far easier to trust than in areas where we've not yet walked and, therefore, not yet needed Him. But I, like the disciples in the boat, face new storms from time to time, and my faith waffles.

But, without fail, no matter what situation comes my way, God shows Himself to be faithful. My prayer now has become, "Lord, I believe, but help my unbelief."

The more I experience life's troubles, the more I experience God because He is always beside me, and each time, my faith grows. Trust Him. He is faithful, and when you have doubt, don't be discouraged; just ask the Lord to help your unbelief. He will, without fail because He is faithful. He will do what He has promised. Watch and see what God will do.

PRAY & BELIEVE

Father, I believe You are good *most* of the time, but something happens, and I begin to doubt. I feel crazy when I go back and forth in my mind. Sometimes, my mind argues with itself, and I wonder if I am crazy! But Lord, remind me that this is normal. It is a constant battle because we are in a sinful world, and I do have an enemy who throttles me with doubt. Jesus, I do believe, but help my unbelief. Show me where those areas are, and teach me to know with certainty that You are good in every circumstance. I need You, every day, to help me, remind me, call me, and not let me go. Amen.

PAUSE TO CONSIDER HIM

What is a recent situation where you argued with yourself, and found yourself doubting if God was good. Did you find in the end that He was good? How can you avoid such a battle next time a situation arises?

_____
_____
_____
_____
_____
_____
_____
_____

Do you believe God is good all the time? Why or why not?

_____
_____
_____
_____
_____
_____

What is your take-away from this lesson?

_____
_____
_____
_____
_____
_____
_____

I Praise You For

-
-
-

The Goodness of God

Oh, taste and see that the Lord is good!
Blessed is the man who takes refuge in him!

Psalm 34:8

Everything changes when we begin to believe the Lord is good. We stop questioning Him and His ways and begin to send roots of trust deep into the soil of our lives. We can easily say "God is Good" when things are going along smoothly or when someone else is facing a trial. But has it become just a phrase? A feel-good quip? An answer to someone else's problems when we have nothing else helpful to say?

Looking at the entirety of the verse, we can see that it is spoken to one who is in trouble because only one facing a trial needs refuge. We don't need refuge in peace but in a storm. It is in a storm we can taste of the Lord. The one who does find their refuge in Him is blessed. It seems odd to be in a storm and be blessed at the same time, but it is true. How?

It's in the tasting. We don't seek God the same way when we are not desperately in need of Him. But when a storm comes, we run to Him. Suddenly, we have time to fall to our knees and pray earnestly. We are tasting the Lord. The peace and confidence that come from the Father are us tasting Him. The storm drives us to Him, where we can take refuge.

Sometimes, our most heartfelt and purest prayers consist of two words: God Help! He hears those prayers and answers them—maybe not always as we would prefer, but how He knows is best. We are blessed in His listening and in His answering. When we know that He is good, we can rest in Him, knowing that no matter what comes, He is our shelter and will answer our plea.

PRAY & BELIEVE

Jesus, I don't want any more storms in my life. I've had more than my share. But I trust You. Storms or not, I know You are for me. I don't know how to taste and see that You are good, so show me what that means. Show me how to find my refuge in You, no matter what. I don't want to run to other vices, whether liquor, shopping, anger, or any other avenue. I want to go to You always! But I can't do that without your help. I am reaching out to You because I know You are reaching out to me, and You will never fail me or let me fall. Thank you for loving me so perfectly. Empower me to love You back. Amen.

PAUSE TO CONSIDER HIM

Do you take refuge in the Lord during difficult times? What does that look like for you? Can you think of a time when you were in the middle of a hard situation yet, you knew you were blessed by the Lord?

_____
_____
_____
_____
_____
_____
_____

How are you a better person today because of what you learned in that experience?

_____
_____
_____
_____
_____
_____

What is your take-away from this lesson?

_____
_____
_____
_____
_____
_____

I Praise You For

-
-
-

An Anchor in the Storm

We have this as a sure and steadfast anchor of the soul, a hope that enters into the inner place behind the curtain,

Hebrews 6:19

If you've ever been on the water in a boat and have reason to stay in a particular location, you know the importance of an anchor. From a small fishing boat to a large ocean liner, the anchor is what keeps the boat fixed, ensuring it does not get pushed by the winds or pulled by the waves.

Storms come, not of our own doing, but we are left with the wreckage. If our families were shattered, or we watched as one parent dragged out their belongings, leaving us behind, the storm was undeniable. Maybe today, you can easily go back to moments when you remember slamming doors or screaming parents, and your emotions are triggered, causing the same feelings today as they did way back then.

Remember that while the storm was not your making, the wreckage it caused is real, and it can be painful, seemingly, without end. But know that you have an anchor even in the storm of another's doing. You have a God that is immovable, and He is holding you close. You have a hope that the wreckage no longer has power over you and that you can heal from it, leaving it behind.

You have a steadfast anchor, even if your family was not that for you. You have a hope that leads you into peace. The past no longer has power over you. Realize it was nothing you had power over then, but you have power over the fallout now. Set it down. Cast all that pain and wreckage overboard and cling tightly to the anchor of your soul.

God can be trusted. He is behind the curtain where peace waits for you and Invites you in. Cling to Him. He is the anchor you need.

PRAY & BELIEVE

You are my anchor, Lord. I know it in my soul, but I tend to forget it when I need to remember it. Jesus, when the world is screaming and my head is spinning, please close off all the noise and let me hear You. Teach me to shut the noise out and focus on who You are. I need so much courage to stand against the noise and strength not to join in. When I am faced with the opportunity to join the anger, pick sides, throw dirt, please help me. Help me be quiet, guard my tongue, show love and kindness, and stand firm, trusting in you. Amen.

PAUSE TO CONSIDER HIM

Think of a few times when the noise was loud and others were trying to pull you to their side. How did you feel? Can you stand firm against it now that you know the Lord is your anchor? Do you see yourself as immoveable?

_____
_____
_____
_____
_____
_____
_____

When the noise is loud, what might the still, small voice of the Lord whisper to you?

_____
_____
_____
_____
_____
_____

What is your take-away from this lesson?

_____
_____
_____
_____
_____
_____

I Praise You For

-
-
-

God Sees

O Lord, you have searched me and known me! You know when I sit down and when I rise up; you discern my thoughts from afar.

Psalm 139:1-2

God didn't have His eyes closed when you were hurting. He was not resting, and He did not turn His back. It may feel like He did, but the older we get, the more we learn that our feelings are not to be trusted. Sometimes, we must stand on what we know to be true instead of what we feel.

God's eyes are on you, no matter where you are or what is happening. He does not watch you with a big stick to smack you on the head when you make a mistake. His eyes are on you because He loves you deeply.

Perhaps you had a parent who was cruel or unkind. Don't judge God by the actions of broken people. We are all broken people; some act out their pain more than others, but God sees even that. He saw you when you were a child, crying in the corner, and He sees you now as an adult, crying silently in your soul. He cares more than you can even imagine. There is nowhere you can hide from Him.

When you step out of bed in the morning, He is there. When you are anxious, He is aware and offers peace. At the midnight hour, when sleep cannot be found and you are pacing the floor with unresolved conflict or fear of tomorrow, He is pacing with you, with His hand outstretched, waiting for you to hold on.

Do it. Grab onto Him, and don't let go. He has known you from before you were a seed in the womb. He formed you. He covered your sin with the blood of His son, and He has a mighty plan for you. Hold onto the God who sees, and no matter what may come, don't let go.

PRAY & BELIEVE

God, I grab onto You with both hands. When I don't feel You, remind me that feelings are flaky and to believe what I know is true, even when my feelings don't align. Lord, You know my thoughts; sometimes, my prayers have no words. Often, I don't know what to say, but You know anyway. You know my heart and understand what I can't put into words. Remind me daily that You are walking with me, pacing with me, holding out Your hand. At the midnight hour, when fear sets in, touch my heart and bring peace. Thank you. Amen.

PAUSE TO CONSIDER HIM

Have you been wrongly judged at times? When? A harder question might be, have you wrongly judged another? We are not the judge, God is the only One who can rightly judge another. Ask Him to help you forgive, and not judge, others in your life.

_____
_____
_____
_____
_____
_____
_____

How did you feel when you were wrongly judged? Can you forgive those who did so?

_____
_____
_____
_____
_____
_____

What is your take-away from this lesson?

_____
_____
_____
_____
_____
_____

I Praise You For

- ●
- ●
- ●

Trusting God with Your Story

Trust in the Lord with all your heart, and do not lean on your own understanding. In all your ways acknowledge him, and he will make straight your paths.

Proverbs 3:5-6

Trusting in the Lord is easy to say but not so easy to do. We have an understanding of the world based on the very limited world we dwell in. Our childhood was the foundation of our world, forming our thoughts and opinions. But our parents, no matter how kind or cruel, based their understanding on their parents' falsehoods, and so it goes all the way back to Adam. This truthful reasoning makes it easy to see that our understanding is severely flawed.

A wise person chooses to trust the One without flaw. The one who created all formed all and wrote the book on our lives is the only one we have any business trusting completely. He knows the paths we are to take because it was His finger that drew them into the dirt.

God planned for our lives. We are not here by mistake but by the divine order of a perfect Creator. He knows the first page of your story and the last. While He did not write the things that hurt you as part of your story, He did allow for them and knew they would make you strong in the end. He can be trusted with your story. God doesn't want us to sit lazily by and do nothing; He wants us to live! And in living, acknowledge Him as we go through this world. Ask Him which way to go when you come to a fork in the road. As you make decisions in your day, seek His wisdom. He will open doors that no man can shut and shut doors you should not be going through.

God can be trusted with your story because He is the author and finisher of your faith. Seek Him first, and He will lead you down the right paths of life.

PRAY & BELIEVE

I choose to trust in You. I know You wrote my story, and the only way I can live it out is to spend time with You and listen for Your leading. Teach me to hear Your voice and give me the desire to seek Your wisdom instead of human wisdom. I want to be wise and walk in Your ways, not mine. You know my desires, Lord, and if You see fit, I ask You to make a way. But if not, I surrender to Your will because I am confident I can trust You with my whole heart. I do want to acknowledge You in all my ways, trusting You to lead me in Your ways. Amen.

PAUSE TO CONSIDER HIM

If you could write the story for your life, what would it look like? Do you believe God has a story for you? Do you believe He planned for your days? Can you surrender your ideas of what life might look like, and receive the story He wrote for you? Tell Him.

_____
_____
_____
_____
_____
_____
_____

What might your life look like if you accepted His story, instead of your own?

_____
_____
_____
_____
_____
_____

What is your take-away from this lesson?

_____
_____
_____
_____
_____
_____

I Praise You For

-
-
-

God in the Broken

*I believe that I shall look upon the goodness of the Lord in
the land of the living! Wait for the Lord; be strong, and
let your heart take courage; wait for the Lord!*

Psalm 27:13-14

Your story is not over; it's only beginning. The things you experienced in your past are done; leave them there and move forward. Stop looking back; you don't live there anymore. Instead, look with joy ahead at where you are going. God is taking you somewhere good, into the land of plenty where the pains from long ago cannot come.

The Lord is good. He was with you in the past and is already in your future, beckoning for you to come. But you cannot live in the present while holding on to the past; one will always win over, and more often than not, the past has the stronger pull. The only way to break its power is to let it go and refuse to pick it back up.

Step out of the land of the old and dead and into the land of the living. It is not easy, but you are stronger than you think. It takes great courage to let go of past pain. To wipe the slate clean, it takes incredible strength to release those who hurt you and no longer hold them accountable. Nothing in our flesh wants to do so, but ask God to give you the desire. He will.

God is with you. He is God in the broken and God in the healing. He wants to heal you from that past burden so you can enjoy fully the present and future He has planned for you. Letting go of what has held you for so long takes time, but in God, there is the courage to do so, and He will help you.

Your best days are ahead, so let the ones behind you go. It might be hard in the moment, but in time, you will look back and find that God was with you all along.

PRAY & BELIEVE

Father, help me to believe that my best days are ahead of me. Give me the desire to let go of my past, with all the hurts and memories, and instead enjoy the present while looking forward to the future. I know You have been with me through it all, and now it's time to let those things of the past go. People make choices because they are broken. Give me strength to stop allowing other people's choices to affect me. Let me see when I am doing that, and remind me of this truth. You alone can heal my scars; I know You are doing that. Bring me closer to You so that others will see how You have changed my heart. Amen.

PAUSE TO CONSIDER HIM

How often do you live in your past; remembering disappointments, rehashing old conversations that were painful? Do you believe that your best days are ahead? Can you trust that God is in your future and ask Him to light the path and lead you?

_____
_____
_____
_____
_____
_____
_____
_____

How would life look differently if you exchanged the past pain for future success?

_____
_____
_____
_____
_____
_____
_____
_____

What is your take-away from this lesson?

_____
_____
_____
_____
_____
_____
_____

I Praise You For

-
-
-

Choosing Thoughts

Finally, brothers, whatever is true, whatever is honorable,
whatever is just, whatever is pure, whatever is lovely, whatever
is commendable, if there is any excellence, if there is anything
worthy of praise, think about these things.

Philippians 4:8

Our thoughts determine our actions, which dictate our outcomes. It is obvious why choosing the right thoughts matters, but in moments of frustration, fear, or anxiety, it is a hard thing to do! We all struggle with this; even the most positive, optimistic person in the world struggles from time to time with choosing the right thoughts.

It might help to look at each word listed in the Scripture above and ponder it. What is an honorable thought? What is commendable? There is a short but seemingly exhaustive list here on which we are to set our thoughts. The Bible reminds us in Proverbs 23:7 that As a man thinks in his heart, so is he. Again, in Proverbs 18:21, We will eat the fruit of our words. Using only these two scriptures, the impact of our thoughts become loud, telling us of their power.

Imagine the impact of choosing thoughts of joy, loveliness, and honor. If we train our minds to think these thoughts, our souls will get in line, causing our words to follow. One cannot dwell on thoughts of anger, unforgiveness, fear, and blame and then open our mouths and expect joy, peace, and love to flow out. Our words mimic our thoughts, and our actions follow. It really is that simple.

What is not simple is training ourselves to replace those negative thoughts with positive ones. It takes time and effort because we are going against a lifetime of habit and what rationally feels like common sense. But change your thoughts and watch your life follow. Tempted to dwell on past pain? Instead, pray for those who cause it; in time, you will notice a change in you!

PRAY & BELIEVE

Father, I have many thoughts that don't align with this Scripture. My thoughts are often negative, and I dwell on painful memories. I want to change that. I want to think of good, joyful, honoring thoughts that are kind and lovely. I cannot do this without Your continual help. Let me hear my thoughts and my words. Open my ears to notice them and the wisdom to know which thoughts can remain and which must leave. Add the courage to stop dwelling on the ones that bring pain and instead set my mind on positive ones that align with this Scripture and Your Word. Amen.

PAUSE TO CONSIDER HIM

What are some patterns of negative thought patterns you notice in your life? Are those rooted in a victim mindset or anger or something else? Can you make a choice to exchange those thoughts for ones of goodness, forgiveness, and honor?

_____
_____
_____
_____
_____
_____
_____

How do you expect your life might improve once you take control of your thoughts?

_____
_____
_____
_____
_____
_____
_____

What is your take-away from this lesson?

_____
_____
_____
_____
_____
_____
_____

I Praise You For

-
-
-

God Says

And after you have suffered a little while, the God of all grace,
who has called you to his eternal glory in Christ, will himself
restore, confirm, strengthen, and establish you.

1 Peter 5:10

We all experience suffering to differing degrees. It's part of living in a fallen world. Sometimes, our suffering is our own doing, as we make terrible decisions and suffer the fallout. Other times, our suffering comes from the bad decisions of others. We cannot control someone else's choices even when the suffering falls upon us. But God...

God Himself will pick us up, clean us off, hold us close, and repair all that has been broken. It is not what others say that determines who we are, but what God says. He will restore us to wholeness. He will confirm and establish us in what He has already created us to be.

Have you thought yourself to be a victim? God says you are victorious. Did someone give you the message that you were not important? God gave His Son to pay your ransom. Have you believed you were a burden? God says He delights in you.

The world, and sometimes those closest to us, will chew us up and spit us out. We live in a broken world with broken people, and we all know that "Hurt people, hurt people." Pray for those who hurt you, intentionally or unintentionally. It seems crazy to do so, but it heals the soul and restores the heart.

Take all those lies the world has said about you and caused you to believe about yourself, and give them to Jesus. Ask Him to show you how He sees you. He will because He is a faithful God and wants to restore you to better than before you were wounded. God created you; who better to trust with the truth of who you truly are?

PRAY & BELIEVE

Lord, I am eternally grateful for Your Word. My life holds some bad memories of past experiences where I felt I was a victim of someone else's decisions. I don't want to hold that, so I give it to You. Take it from me, and when I am tempted to slip back into that mindset, remind me I am not a victim, but because of You, I can live in victory. Soften the memories that I struggle to give up and give me the desire to want to lay them down and leave them with You. Thank you for being victorious at the cross so I can be a victor in my life. Amen.

PAUSE TO CONSIDER HIM

Who has the world told you that you are? Is that accurate according the the bible?
Who does God say you are? Can you exchange the world's view for the truth of God?
He says you are excellent, the apple of His eye, the one who He loves.

_____
_____
_____
_____
_____
_____
_____
_____

How would your life improve if you replaced the world's view of you, with God's?

_____
_____
_____
_____
_____
_____
_____

What is your take-away from this lesson?

_____
_____
_____
_____
_____
_____

I Praise You For

-
-
-

www.ingramcontent.com/pod-product-compliance
Lightning Source LLC
Chambersburg PA
CBHW041630140626
46547CB00032B/2470